Xmas 95

To Dick & Lois,

With Love

From
Peter & Anna.

BANJO PATERSON

Under Sunny Skies

Joseph Wolinski, *Molonglo River*, 1912. National Library of Australia.

BANJO PATERSON

Under Sunny Skies

ILLUSTRATED WITH AUSTRALIAN LANDSCAPE PAINTINGS

Selected by Margaret Olds

NATIONAL
BOOK DISTRIBUTORS AND PUBLISHERS

Published by
National Book Distributors and Publishers
3/2 Aquatic Drive, Frenchs Forest, New South Wales, 2086, Australia

Devised and produced for the publishers by
Murray Child & Company Pty Ltd
64 Suffolk Avenue, Collaroy, New South Wales, 2097, Australia
Designed by Murray Child and Emma Seymour
This collection of poems and paintings
© Murray Child & Company Pty Ltd, 1994
© Design, Murray Child & Company Pty Ltd,1994
Digital colour separation and film by Type Scan, Adelaide
Printed by Southbank Book, Melbourne

National Library of Australia Cataloguing-in-Publication Data

Paterson, A. B. (Andrew Barton), 1864–1941.
[Poems, Selections]. The Banjo Paterson collection.

ISBN 1 863436 023 2 (set).
ISBN 1 86436 030 5 (v.1).
ISBN 1 86436 031 3 (v.2).

1. Paterson, A. B. (Andrew Barton), 1864–1941. In the
droving days. II. Paterson, A. B. (Andrew Barton), 1864–
1941. Under sunny skies.
III. Olds, Margaret. IV. Title. V. Title: Under sunny skies.
VI. Title: In the droving days.

A821.2

Contents

Introduction	6
Barney Devine	8
The Open Steeplechase	10
A Mountain Station	13
A Bunch of Roses	16
The Wind's Message	18
Waltzing Matilda	20
How the Favourite Beat Us	22
It's Grand	25
Saltbush Bill, J.P.	27
Road to Gundagai	32
The Mountain Squatter	34
General Drought and General Rain	37
By the Grey Gulf-water	40
To George Lambert	42
Song of Murray's Brigade	43
A Ballad of Ducks	45

Introduction

Following the success of his collection of poems *The Man from Snowy River and Other Verses*, "Banjo" Paterson went to Queensland late in 1895 to stay with friends on a cattle station near Winton. There he wrote what was to become Australia's national song, "Waltzing Matilda". This poem has become a folk icon and part of the Australian identity. It has attached at least two tunes to itself and survives in a number of slightly different versions—and of course each of us favours the version we learnt as a child and insist that is the right version! Absorption into a living and vital folk tradition in this way is perhaps the highest compliment generations of Australians could pay Paterson.

In the following years Paterson turned to journalism and for the next thirty years he worked as both a journalist and a poet. In 1899 he sailed for South Africa and covered the South African War for the *Sydney Morning Herald* and the *Age*. In 1901 he travelled to China to cover the Boxer Rebellion. All the time he continued to write poetry and in 1902 *Rio Grande's Last Race, and Other Verses* was published. In 1905 he published a collection called *Old Bush Songs* and in 1906 *An Outback Marriage* (a novel) appeared.

With the outbreak of the First World War Paterson went to Europe hoping to be a war correspondent but he was unable to get to the front. He returned to Australia, enlisted in the Remount Service, which provided horses for the cavalry, and served in the Middle East. In 1917 *Saltbush Bill, J. P. and Other Verses* was published.

After the war he returned to Australia and continued with journalism and his other writing. In 1923 *Collected Verse*, which contains most of his poems and has reprinted many times, appeared. And in 1933, *The Animals Noah Forgot*, a collection of verse for children was published. He died in Sydney on 5 February 1941.

Paterson's legacy is a verse collection that typifies the spirit of an era. His work is representative of a generation of writers and artists who were the image makers at a time when the Australian character (and, indeed, the nation itself) was emerging.

MARGARET OLDS

Barney Devine

Tune: 'Paddy McGhee'

Where are you roving now, Barney Devine,
Shearing or droving now, what is your line?
Oh, but it's years since the last that we heard,
Never a mailman has brought us a word.

Chorus
Anyhow, anywhere, country or town,
Making the money or knocking it down.
Drought or wet weather, in rain or in shine,
Here's a long life to you, Barney Devine!

Say, are you shearing away in the west,
You that were always the fastest and best,
Shearing a hundred with never a scratch!
Where was the shearer could turn out their match?

Out on the cattle camps waiting for light,
Watching the stock in the hush of the night,
Singing your songs of the bush and its ways,
Telling your tales of the wandering days.

Far, far away though you happen to roam,
Ne'er you'll forget them the old folks at home,
Sadly they wait for a word or a line
Won't you come back to them, Barney Devine?

Duncan Cooper, 1813 or 14–1904, *On the plains near Challicum*, watercolour 12.7 x 19 cm, *The Challicum Sketch Book*. National Library of Australia.

The Open Steeplechase

I had ridden over hurdles up the country once or twice,
By the side of Snowy River with a horse they called "The Ace".
And we brought him down to Sydney, and our rider, Jimmy Rice,
Got a fall and broke his shoulder, so they nabbed me in a trice—
Me, that never wore the colours, for the Open Steeplechase.

"Make the running," said the trainer, "it's your only chance
    whatever,
Make it hot from start to finish, for the old black horse can stay,
And just think of how they'll take it, when they hear on Snowy
    River
That the country boy was plucky, and the country horse was
    clever.
You must ride for old Monaro and the mountain boys today."

"Are you ready?" said the starter, as we held the horses back,
All ablazing with impatience, with excitement all aglow;
Before us like a ribbon stretched the steeplechasing track,
And the sunrays glistened brightly on the chestnut and the black
As the starter's words came slowly, "Are—you—ready? Go!"

Well, I scarcely knew we'd started, I was stupid-like with wonder
Till the field closed up beside me and a jump appeared ahead.
And we flew it like a hurdle, not a baulk and not a blunder,
As we charged it all together, and it fairly whistled under,
And then some were pulled behind me and a few shot out and led.

So we ran for half the distance, and I'm making no pretences
When I tell you I was feeling very nervous-like and queer,
For those jockeys rode like demons; you would think they'd lost
    their senses

If you saw them rush their horses at those rasping five foot
    fences—
And in place of making running I was falling to the rear.

Till a chap came racing past me on a horse they called "The
    Quiver",
And said he, "My country joker, are you going to give it best?
Are you frightened of the fences? Does their stoutness make you
    shiver?
Have they come to breeding cowards by the side of Snowy River?
Are there riders on Monaro?—" but I never heard the rest.

T. H. Lyttleton, 1826–1876, *Steeplechase at Gonn Station, Victoria*, 1869. Purchased 1979.
Warrnambool Art Gallery.

For I drove The Ace and sent him just as fast as he could pace it,
At the big black line of timber stretching fair across the track,
And he shot beside The Quiver. "Now," said I, "my boy, we'll race
    it.
You can come with Snowy River if you're only game to face it;
Let us mend the pace a little and we'll see who cries a crack."

So we raced away together, and we left the others standing,
And the people cheered and shouted as we settled down to ride,
And we clung beside The Quiver. At his taking off and landing
I could see his scarlet nostril and his mighty ribs expanding,
And The Ace stretched out in earnest and we held him stride for
    stride.

But the pace was so terrific that they soon ran out their tether—
They were rolling in their gallop, they were fairly blown and
    beat—
But they both were game as pebbles—neither one would show
    the feather.
And we rushed them at the fences, and they cleared them both
    together,
Nearly every time they clouted but they somehow kept their feet.

Then the last jump rose before us, and they faced it game as
    ever—
We were both at spur and whipcord, fetching blood at every
    bound—
And above the people's cheering and the cries of "Ace" and
    "Quiver",
I could hear the trainer shouting, "One more run for Snowy River".
Then we struck the jump together and came smashing to the
    ground.

Well, The Quiver ran to blazes, but The Ace stood still and waited,
Stood and waited like a statue while I scrambled on his back.
There was no one next or near me for the field was fairly slated,
So I cantered home a winner with my shoulder dislocated,
While the man that rode The Quiver followed limping down the
    track.

And he shook my hand and told me that in all his days he never
Met a man who rode more gamely, and our last set to was prime,
And we wired them on Monaro how we chanced to beat The
    Quiver.
And they sent us back an answer, "Good old sort from Snowy
    River;
Send us word each race you start in and we'll back you every
    time."

A Mountain Station

I bought a run a while ago,
    On country rough and ridgy,
Where wallaroos and wombats grow—
    The Upper Murrumbidgee.
The grass is rather scant, it's true,
    But this a fair exchange is,
The sheep can see a lovely view
    By climbing up the ranges.

And "She-oak Flat" 's the station's name,
    I'm not surprised at that, sirs:
The oaks were there before I came,
    And I supplied the flat, sirs.
A man would wonder how it's done,

The stock so soon decreases—
They sometimes tumble off the run
    And break themselves to pieces.

I've tried to make expenses meet,
    But wasted all my labours,
The sheep the dingoes didn't eat
    Were stolen by the neighbours.
They stole my pears—my native pears—
    Those thrice-convicted felons,
And ravished from me unawares
    My crop of paddymelons.

And sometimes under sunny skies,
    Without an explanation,
The Murrumbidgee used to rise
    And overflow the station.
But this was caused (as now I know)
    When summer sunshine glowing
Had melted all Kiandra's snow
    And set the river going.

And in the news, perhaps you read:
    "Stock passings. Puckawidgee,
Fat cattle: Seven hundred head
    Swept down the Murrumbidgee;
Their destination's quite obscure,
    But somehow, there's a notion,
Unless the river falls, they're sure
    To reach the Southern Ocean."

W. C. Piguenit, Australia, 1863–1914, *Arthur Range and plains from the Flying Ant Hill, looking south*, 1874, watercolour, pencil on paper 25.8 x 36 cm. National Gallery of Australia, Canberra.

So after that I'll give it best;
   No more with Fate I'll battle.
I'll let the river take the rest,
   For those were all my cattle.
And with one comprehensive curse
   I close my brief narration,
And advertise it in my verse—
   "For Sale! A Mountain Station".

A Bunch of Roses

Roses ruddy and roses white,
    What are the joys that my heart discloses?
Sitting alone in the fading light
Memories come to me here to-night
    With the wonderful scent of the big red roses.

Memories come as the daylight fades
    Down on the hearth where the firelight dozes;
Flicker and flutter the lights and shades,
And I see the face of a queen of maids
    Whose memory comes with the scent of roses.

John Glover, Australia, 1767–1849, *A view of the artist's house and garden, in Mills Plains, Van Diemen's Land*, 1835, oil on canvas 76.4 x 114.4 cm. Morgan Thomas Bequest Fund 1951. Art Gallery of South Australia.

Visions arise of a scene of mirth,
    And a ballroom belle that superbly poses—
A queenly woman of queenly worth,
And I am the happiest man on earth
    With a single flower from a bunch of roses.

Only her memory lives tonight—
    God in His wisdom her young life closes;
Over her grave may the turf be light,
Cover her coffin with roses white—
    She was always fond of the big white roses.

Such are visions that fade away—
    Man proposes and God disposes;
Look in the glass and I see to-day
Only an old man, worn and grey,
    Bending his head to a bunch of roses.

The Wind's Message

There came a whisper down the Bland between the dawn and
   dark,
Above the tossing of the pines, above the river's flow;
It stirred the boughs of giant gums and stalwart ironbark;
It drifted where the wild ducks played amid the swamps below;
It brought a breath of mountain air from off the hills of pine,
A scent of eucalyptus trees in honey-laden bloom;
And drifting, drifting far away along the southern line
It caught from leaf and grass and fern a subtle strange perfume.
It reached the toiling city folk, but few there were that heard—
The rattle of their busy life had choked the whisper down;
And some but caught a fresh-blown breeze with scent of pine that
   stirred
A thought of blue hills far away beyond the smoky town;
And others heard the whisper pass, but could not understand
The magic of the breeze's breath that set their hearts aglow,
Nor how the roving wind could bring across the Overland
A sound of voices silent now and songs of long ago.

But some that heard the whisper clear were filled with vague
   unrest;
The breeze had brought its message home, they could not fixed
   abide;
Their fancies wandered all the day towards the blue hills' breast,
Towards the sunny slopes that lie along the riverside,
The mighty rolling western plains are very fair to see,
Where waving to the passing breeze the silver myalls stand,
But fairer are the giant hills, all rugged though they be,
From which the two great rivers rise that run along the Bland.

Unknown artist, *Australian Bush*, c. 1850. The Rex Nan Kivell Collection, National Library of Australia.

Oh! rocky range and rugged spur and river running clear,
That swings around the sudden bends with swirl of snow-white
    foam,
Though we, your sons, are far away, we sometimes seem to hear
The message that the breezes bring to call the wanderers home.
The mountain peaks are white with snow that feeds a thousand
    rills,
Along the river banks the maize grows tall on virgin land,
And we shall live to see once more those sunny southern hills,
And strike once more the bridle track that leads along the Bland.

Waltzing Matilda

Once a jolly swagman camped by a billabong,
    Under the shade of a coolibah tree,
And he sang as he watched and waited 'til his billy boiled,
    "Who'll come a-waltzing Matilda with me—
Waltzing Matilda, waltzing Matilda, who'll come a-waltzing
    Matilda with me?"
And he sang as he watched and waited 'til his billy boiled,
    "Who'll come a-waltzing Matilda with me?"

Down came a jumbuck to drink at the billabong
    Up jumped the swagman and grabbed him with glee,
And he sang, as he stowed that jumbuck in his tucker-bag,
    "Who'll come a-waltzing Matilda with me?
Waltzing Matilda, waltzing Matilda, who'll come a-waltzing
    Matilda with me?"
And he sang as he stowed that jumbuck in his tucker-bag,
    "Who'll come a-waltzing Matilda with me?"

Up came the squatter, mounted on his thoroughbred,
    Down came the troopers—one, two, three—
"Whose is the jolly jumbuck, you've got in your tucker-bag?
    You'll come a-waltzing Matilda with me.
Waltzing Matilda, waltzing Matilda, who'll come a-waltzing
    Matilda with me?
Whose is the jolly jumbuck you've got in your tucker-bag.
    You'll come a-waltzing Matilda with me."

Duncan Cooper, 1813 or 14–1904, *Challicum, First station and huts, January 1842, Early summer*, watercolour 18.6 x 28.1 cm, *The Challicum Sketch Book*. National Library of Australia.

Up jumped the swagman, and sprang into the billabong,
 "You'll never take me alive!" said he.
And his ghost may be heard, as we pass by that billabong,
 "Who'll come a-waltzing Matilda with me?
Waltzing Matilda, waltzing Matilda,
 Who'll come a-waltzing Matilda with me?"
And his ghost may be heard, as we pass by that billabong,
 "Who'll come a-waltzing Matilda with me?"

How the Favourite Beat Us

"Aye," said the boozer, "I tell you it's true, sir,
   I once was a punter with plenty of pelf,
But gone is my glory, I'll tell you the story
   How I stiffened my horse and got stiffened myself.

" 'Twas a mare called the Cracker, I came down to back her,
   But found she was favourite all of a rush,
The folk just did pour on to lay six to four on,
   And several bookies were killed in the crush.

"It seems old Tomato was stiff, though a starter;
    They reckoned him fit for the Caulfield to keep.
The Bloke and the Donah were scratched by their owner,
    He only was offered three-fourths of the sweep.

"We knew Salamander was slow as a gander,
    The mare could have beat him the length of the straight,
And old Manumission was out of condition,
    And most of the others were running off weight.

"No doubt someone 'blew it', for everyone knew it
    The bets were all gone, and I muttered in spite,
'If I can't get a copper, by Jingo, I'll stop her,
    Let the public fall in, it will serve the brutes right.'

George Lambert, Australia,
1873–1930. Untitled (The Tirranna
Picnic Race Meeting), 1929, oil on
canvas 76.5 x 152.5. The Russell
and Mab Grimwade Bequest
1973. The University of Melbourne
Collection.

"I said to the jockey, 'Now, listen, my cocky,
    You watch as you're cantering down by the stand,
I'll wait where that toff is and give you the office,
    You're only to win if I lift up my hand.'

"I then tried to back her—'What price is the Cracker?'
    'Our books are all full, sir' each bookie did swear;
My mind, then, I made up, my fortune I played up
    I bet every shilling against my own mare.

"I strolled to the gateway, the mare in the straight way
    Was shifting and dancing, and pawing the ground,
The boy saw me enter and wheeled for his canter,
    When a darned great mosquito came buzzing around.

"They breed 'em at Hexham, it's risky to vex 'em
    They suck a man dry at a sitting, no doubt,
But just as the mare passed, he fluttered my hair past,
    I lifted my hand, and I flattened him out.

"I was stunned when they started, the mare simply darted
    Away to the front when the flag was let fall,
For none there could match her, and none tried to catch her—
    She finished a furlong in front of them all.

"You bet that I went for the boy, whom I sent for
    The moment he weighed and came out of the stand—
'Who paid you to win it? Come, own up this minute.'
    'Lord love yer,' said he, 'why, you lifted your hand.'

" 'Twas true, by St Peter, that cursed 'musketeer'
    Had broke me so broke that I hadn't a brown,
And you'll find the best course is when dealing with horses
    To win when you're able, and *keep your hands down*."

It's Grand

It's grand to be a squatter
    And sit upon a post,
And watch your little ewes and lambs
    A-giving up the ghost.

It's grand to be a 'cockie'
    With wife and kids to keep,
And find an all-wise Providence
    Has mustered all your sheep.

It's grand to be a western man,
    With shovel in your hand,
To dig your little homestead out
    From underneath the sand.

It's grand to be a shearer,
    Along the Darling side,
And pluck the wool from stinking sheep
    That some days since have died.

It's grand to be a rabbit
    And breed to all is blue,
And then to die in heaps because
    There's nothing left to chew.

It's grand to be a Minister
    And travel like a swell,
And tell the central district folk
    To go to—Inverell.

Elioth Gruner, Australia, 1882–1939, *Spring Frost*, 1919, oil on canvas 131 x 178.7 cm. Gift of F. G. White 1939. Art Gallery of New South Wales.

It's grand to be a Socialist
　　And lead the bold array
That marches to prosperity
　　At seven bob a day.

It's grand to be an unemployed
　　And lie in the Domain,
And wake up every second day
　　And go to sleep again.

It's grand to borrow English tin
　　To pay for wharves and Rocks,
And then to find it isn't in
　　The little money-box.

It's grand to be a democrat
    And toady to the mob,
For fear that if you told the truth
    They'd hunt you from your job.

It's grand to be a lot of things
    In this fair southern land,
But if the Lord would send us rain,
    That would indeed, be grand!

Saltbush Bill, J.P.

Beyond the land where Leichhardt went,
    Beyond Sturt's western track,
The rolling tide of change has sent
    Some strange J.P.s out back.

And Saltbush Bill, grown old and grey,
    And worn with want of sleep,
Received the news in camp one day
    Behind the travelling sheep,

That Edward Rex, confiding in
    His known integrity,
By hand and seal on parchment skin
    Had made him a J.P.

He read the news with eager face
    But found no word of pay.
"I'd like to see my sister's place
    And kids on Christmas Day.

"I'd like to see green grass again,
    And watch clear water run,
Away from this unholy plain,
    And flies, and dust, and sun."

At last one little clause he found
    That might some hope inspire,
"A magistrate may charge a pound
    For inquest on a fire."

A big blacks' camp was built close by
    And Saltbush Bill, says he,
"I think that camp might well supply
    A job for a J.P."

That night, by strange coincidence,
    A most disastrous fire
Destroyed the country residence
    Of Jacky Jack, Esquire.

'Twas mostly leaves, and bark, and dirt;
    The party most concerned
Appeared to think it wouldn't hurt
    If forty such were burned.

Quite otherwise thought Saltbush Bill,
    Who watched the leaping flame.
"The home is small", said he, "but still
    The principle's the same.

" 'Midst palaces though you should roam,
    Or follow pleasure's tracks,

You'll find", he said, "no place like home,
    At least like Jacky Jack's.

"Tell every man in camp 'Come quick',
    Tell every black Maria,
I give tobacco half a stick—
    Hold inquest long-a fire."

Each juryman received a name
    Well suited to a Court.
"Long Jack" and "Stumpy Bill" became
    "John Long" and "William Short".

While such as "Tarpot", "Bullock Dray",
    And "Tommy Wait-a-While",
Became, for ever and a day,
    "Scott", "Dickens", and "Carlyle".

And twelve good sable men and true
    Were soon engaged upon
The conflagration that o'erthrew
    The home of John A. John.

Their verdict, "Burnt by act of fate",
    They scarcely had returned
When, just behind the magistrate,
    Another humpy burned!

The jury sat again and drew
    Another stick of plug.
Said Saltbush Bill, "It's up to you
    Put some one long-a jug."

"I'll camp the sheep", he said, "and sift
   The evidence about."
For quite a week he couldn't shift,
   The way the fires broke out.

The jury thought the whole concern
   As good as any play.
They used to "take him oath" and earn
   Three sticks of plug a day.

At last the tribe lay down to sleep
   Homeless, beneath a tree;
And onward with his travelling sheep
   Went Saltbush Bill, J.P.

J. B. Goodrich, *Blue Mountains bivouac*, c. 1850. The Rex Nan Kivell Collection, National Library of Australia.

The sheep delivered, safe and sound,
    His horse to town he turned,
And drew some five-and-twenty pound
    For fees that he had earned.

And where Monaro's ranges hide
    Their little farms away,
His sister's children by his side,
    He spent his Christmas Day.

The next J.P. that went outback
    Was shocked, or pained, or both
At hearing every pagan black
    Repeat the juror's oath.

No matter though he turned and fled
    They followed faster still,
"You make it inkwich, boss," they said
    "All same like Saltbush Bill."

They even said they'd let him see
    The fires originate.
When he refused they said that he
    Was "No good magistrate."

And out beyond Sturt's western track,
    And Leichhardt's furthest tree,
They wait till fate shall send them back
    Their Saltbush Bill J.P.

Road to Gundagai

The mountain road goes up and down,
From Gundagai to Tumut town.

And branching off there runs a track,
Across the foothills grim and black,

Across the plains and ranges grey
To Sydney city far away.

It came by chance one day that I
From Tumut rode to Gundagai.

And reached about the evening tide
The crossing where the roads divide;

And, waiting at the crossing place,
I saw a maiden fair of face,

With eyes of deepest violet blue,
And cheeks to match the rose in hue—

The fairest maids Australia knows
Are bred among the mountain snows.

Then, fearing I might go astray,
I asked if she could show the way.

Her voice might well a man bewitch—
Its tones so supple, deep, and rich.

"The tracks are clear," she made reply,
"And this goes down to Sydney town,
And that one goes to Gundagai."

Then slowly, looking coyly back,
She went along the Sydney track.

And I for one was well content
To go the road the lady went;

But round the turn a swain she met—
The kiss she gave him haunts me yet!

I turned and travelled with a sigh
The lonely road to Gundagai.

Henry A. Fullwood, *Landscape in NSW*, c. 1904. National Library of Australia.

The Mountain Squatter

Here in my mountain home,
    On rugged hills and steep,
I sit and watch you come,
    Oh Riverina Sheep!

You come from fertile plains
    Where saltbush (sometimes) grows,
And flats that (when it rains)
    Will blossom like the rose.

But when the summer sun
    Gleams down like burnished brass
You have to leave your run
    And hustle off for grass.

'Tis then that—forced to roam—
    You come to where I keep,
Here in my mountain home,
    A boarding-house for sheep.

Around me where I sit
    The wary wombat goes,
A beast of little wit
    But what he knows, he *knows*.

The very same remark
    Applies to me also,
I don't give out a spark,
    But what I know, I *know*.

My brain perhaps would show
   No convolutions deep;
But anyhow I know
   The way to handle sheep.

These Riverina cracks,
   They do not care to ride
The half-inch hanging tracks
   Along the mountain side.

Their horses shake with fear
   When loosened boulders go,
With leaps, like startled deer,
   Down to the gulfs below.

Their very dogs will shirk,
   And drop their tails in fright
When asked to go and work
   A mob that's out of sight.

My little collie pup
   Works silently and wide,
You'll see her climbing up
   Along the mountain side.

As silent as a fox
   You'll see her come and go
A shadow through the rocks
   Where ash and messmate grow.

Then, lost to sight and sound
   Behind some rugged steep,
She works her way around
   And gathers up the sheep.

Joseph Wolinski, *Molonglo River*, 1912. National Library of Australia.

And working wide and shy,
   She holds them rounded up.
The cash ain't coined to buy
   That little collie pup.

And so I draw a screw
   For self and dog and keep
To boundary ride for you,
   Oh Riverina Sheep!

And when the autumn rain
   Has made the herbage grow,
You travel off again,
   And glad—no doubt—to go!

But some are left behind
    Around the mountain's spread,
For those we cannot find
    We put them down as dead.

But when we say *adieu*
    And close the boarding job,
I always find a few
    Fresh earmarks in my mob.

So what with those I sell,
    And what with those I keep,
You pay me pretty well,
    Oh Riverina Sheep!

It's up to me to shout
    Before we say goodbye—
"Here's to a howlin' drought
    All west of Gundagai!"

General Drought and General Rain

Parched are the plains and bare,
Dusty and eaten out:
Animals everywhere
Perish in dump despair;
For the land is held in the iron grip
Of the enemy General Drought!

Who shall deliver us?
Who shall assuage our pain?
Men in their bitter grief,

Pray that they get relief,
That help may come from the friendly hand
Of our ally, General Rain.

Look at those flying mists
Sweeping across the plain!
These are the lads of the Light Brigade,
Light but fearless and undismayed;
They are the van of the first attack
Of the valiant General Rain.

Now are the Light Brigade
Baffled and beaten back:
But the blast of the rain-wind fifing clear,
Rallies its forces far and near
On to the grand attack.

Out of the stormy south
To the sound of the thunder's drum,
Peal upon peal, and crash on crash,
To the heliograph of the lightning flash,
The big battalions come!

Look at those big black clouds,
Gathering out at sea!
Never the swiftest war horse yet
Moved as they move, all stern and set,
On to their victory!

Never a Maxim Gun
Shoots like the stinging hail,
Never the blast of a fifer rings
Clear as the call that the storm wind sings

Peter Purves Smith, Australia, 1891–1974, *Drought*, 1939, gouache on paper 48.8 x 40.2 cm. Gift of an anonymous donor 1986. National Gallery of Australia, Canberra. Reproduced with the kind permission of Lady Drysdale.

As the foe begins to fail.
Now may our thanks ascend
Over the smiling plain.
Thanks let us give that the foe falls back,
Crushed by the might of the fierce attack
Of the valiant General Rain.

By the Grey Gulf-water

Far to the northward there lies a land,
    A wonderful land that the winds blow over,
And none may fathom nor understand
    The charm it holds for the restless rover;
A great grey chaos—a land half made,
    Where endless space is and no life stirreth;
And the soul of a man will recoil afraid
    From the sphinx-like visage that Nature weareth.
But old Dame Nature, though scornful, craves
    Her dole of death and her share of slaughter;
Many indeed are the nameless graves
    Where her victims sleep by the Grey Gulf-water.

Slowly and slowly those grey streams glide,
    Drifting along with a languid motion,
Lapping the reed beds on either side,
    Wending their way to the Northern Ocean.
Grey are the plains where the emus pass
    Silent and slow, with their staid demeanour;
Over the dead men's graves the grass
    Maybe is waving a trifle greener.

Down in the world where men toil and spin
    Dame Nature smiles as man's hand has taught her;
Only the dead men her smiles can win
    In the great lone land by the Grey Gulf-water.
For the strength of man is an insect's strength,
    In the face of that mighty plain and river,
And the life of a man is a moment's length
    To the life of the stream that will run for ever.
And so it cometh they take no part
    In a small-world worries; each hardy rover
Rideth abroad and is light of heart,
    With the plains around and the blue sky over.
And up in the heavens the brown lark sings
    The songs that the strange wild land has taught her;
Full of thanksgiving her sweet song rings—
    And I wish I were back by the Grey Gulf-water.

To George Lambert

An Essay on Australian Art and Literature (written 1929)
In recognition of Lambert's really excellent portrait of Mrs Paterson

Come all ye men of paint and pen,
   Who toil with hand and brain.
Forsake the town and take the brown
   And dusty roads again,
The tracks that we old-timers know,
Who showed you all the way to go
With Clancy of the Overflow
   Across the Black Soil Plain.

George Lambert, Australia, 1873–1930. *Across the Black Soil Plains*, 1899, oil on canvas 91.6 x 305.5 cm. Purchased 1899. Art Gallery of New South Wales.

Song of Murray's Brigade

Small birds singing in the tree tops tell
   Where runs the river of my home
And the wistful wishing of the folk who love us well
   And follow us wherever we may roam.

And our hearts go back to the folk beside the river
To the land where the sheep and cattle roam
It's a long, long job, but we'll finish it together
   For every mile we travel leads us home.

No songs greet us for the birds are mute
   The aeroplane's the only thing to fly
Upward to the pilot send a special brand salute
   For we may need him badly bye and bye.

Jessie E. Scarvell, *Landscape, c.* 1876. The Rex Nan Kivell Collection, National Library of Australia.

Soldiers singing as their fancies come
   New songs, old songs, they sang another day
Thus they sing and march to the beating of the drum
   Till orders come to put the drums away.

And our hearts go back to the folk beside the river
   To the land where the sheep and cattle roam
It's a long, long job, but we'll finish it together
   For every mile we travel leads us home.

A Ballad of Ducks

The railway rattled and roared and swung
With jolting carriage and bumping trucks.
The sun, like a billiard red ball, hung
In the western sky: and the tireless tongue
Of the wild-eyed man in the corner told
This terrible tale of the days of old,
And the party that ought to have kept the ducks.

"Well, it ain't all joy bein' on the land
With an overdraft that'd knock you flat;
And the rabbits have pretty well took command;
But the hardest thing for a man to stand
Is the feller who says, 'Well, I told you so!
You should ha' done this way, don't you know!'
I could lay a bait for a man like that.

"The grasshoppers struck us in ninety-one
And what they leave—well, it ain't *de luxe.*
But a growlin' fault-findin' son of a gun
Who'd lent some money to stock our run—
I said they'd eaten what grass we had—
Says he, 'Your management's very bad,
You had a right to have kept some ducks!'

"To have kept some ducks! And the place was white!
Wherever you went you had to tread
On grasshoppers guzzlin' day and night;
And when with a swoosh they rose in flight,
If you didn't look out for yourself they'd fly
Like bullets into your open eye
And knock it out of the back of your head.

Abram Louis Buvelot, 1814–1888, Australia. *Waterpool at Coleraine,* 1869, oil on canvas 106.7 x 152.4 cm. Purchased with the assistance of a Government Grant 1870. National Gallery of Victoria.

"There isn't a turkey or goose or swan,
Or a duck that quacks, or a hen that clucks,
Can make a difference on a run
When a grasshopper plague has once begun;
'If you'd finance us,' I says, 'I'd buy
Ten thousand emus and have a try;
The job,' I says, 'is too big for ducks!

" 'You must fetch a duck when you come to stay;
A great big duck—a Muscovy toff—
Ready and fit,' I says, 'for the fray;
And if the grasshoppers come our way

You turn your duck into the lucerne patch,
And I'd be ready to make a match
That the grasshoppers eats his feathers off!'

"He came to visit us by and by,
And it just so happened one day in spring
A kind of cloud came over the sky—
A wall of grasshoppers nine miles high,
And nine miles thick, and nine hundred wide,
Flyin' in regiments, side by side,
And eatin' up every living thing.

"All day long, like a shower of rain,
You'd hear 'em smackin' against the wall,
Tap, tap, tap, on the window pane,
And they'd rise and jump at the house again
Till their crippled carcases piled outside.
But what did it matter if thousands died—
A million wouldn't be missed at all.

"We were drinkin' grasshoppers—so to speak—
Till we skimmed their carcases off the spring;
And they fell so thick in the station creek
They choked the waterholes all the week.
There was scarcely room for a trout to rise,
And they'd only take artificial flies—
They got so sick of the real thing.

"An Arctic snowstorm was beat to rags
When the hoppers rose for their morning flight
With a flapping noise like a million flags:
And the kitchen chimney was stuffed with bags
For they'd fall right into the fire, and fry

Till the cook sat down and began to cry—
And never a duck or a fowl in sight!

"We strolled across to the railroad track—
Under a cover, beneath some trucks,
I sees a feather and hears a quack;
I stoops and I pulls the tarpaulin back—
Every duck in the place was there,
No good to them was the open air.
'Mister', I says, 'There's your blanky ducks!' "